INDIAN FESTIVALS

Troll Associates

INDIAN FESTIVALS

by Keith Brandt

Illustrated by George Guzzi

Troll Associates

Library of Congress Cataloging in Publication Data

Brandt, Keith, (date)
   Indian festivals.

   Summary: Gives brief descriptions of the major festi-
vals celebrated by various Indian tribes throughout North
America.
   1. Indians of North America—Rites and ceremonies—
Juvenile literature.   2. Indians of North America—Dances
—Juvenile literature.   [1. Indians of North America—
Rites and Ceremonies]   I. Guzzi, George, ill.   II. Title.
E98.R3B73   1984   394.2'08997   84-2644
ISBN 0-8167-0182-2 (lib. bdg.)
ISBN 0-8167-0183-0 (pbk.)

10 9 8 7 6 5 4 3 2 1

Apache dance ceremony

The North American Indians had strong feelings about the earth. They believed that they were lucky to share in the bounty of the land. And they believed that they shared this bounty with all the plants and animals around them. To show their thankfulness and to show respect for the forces of nature, the Indians held many festivals and celebrations.

7

Bean-planting ceremony

The festivals were different from place to place because throughout North America the land was different, the Indian tribes were different, and the way each tribe lived was different from the others.

8

Warrior Dance

Tribes that were farmers celebrated the harvests. Tribes that were hunters celebrated the abundance of the animal life and the seasons of the hunt. Warlike tribes held festivals in honor of a great victory.

Many tribes celebrated marriages, births, deaths, and the coming of age of their young people. There were many religious reasons for festivals. There were also feasts and festivals just to share food, friendship, and fun.

The Iroquois Indians of the Eastern Woodlands held six large public festivals every year. At these they gave thanks for the plants that grew from the earth, because they believed they were gifts from the Great Spirit.

The first festival of the year, held in midwinter, was the seven-day Dream, or New Year, Festival. It was also called the Festival of the White Dog. This was because a white dog was sacrificed to the Great Spirit during the festival.

The Iroquois believed that the white dog traveled to the skies as their messenger. Throughout the seven days of the festival they enjoyed games and dances, and important members of the tribe visited each

home. There, they would stir the cooking fire to symbolize the coming spring and the warmth and the life it would bring once again.

The next festival of the Iroquois, held in early March, was the Maple Festival. At this time of year the sap began to flow in the maple trees. The Iroquois gave thanks for this source of sugar by holding feasts and war dances. The war dance was a show of strength and energy at a time when the earth was showing *its* strength and energy.

Later in the spring, the Iroquois celebrated the Planting Festival. It marked the time when they should start to plant the corn. During the Planting Festival they prayed that the Great Spirit would bless the seeds they put into the soil.

Just before summer, the Iroquois held a Strawberry Festival to give thanks for the first fruits of the season.

In mid-summer there was a Green Corn Festival. This was highlighted by games, dances, sports, feasting, and prayers in honor of the "three sisters"—corn, beans, and squash.

Finally, in the autumn, the Iroquois enjoyed a big harvest thanksgiving festival. It celebrated all that the Great Spirit had given them throughout the year.

The Algonquin Indians of the Eastern Woodlands were hunters. Most of the time they lived in very small villages. But at least once or twice a year, the Algonquins came together for a big powwow, or meeting.

At this meeting they held feasts, dances, and games. The powwow was more of a social and political get-together than a religious festival. The Algonquins did make offerings to the spirit world, but they did so as individuals, not as a group.

A typical Algonquin festival was held simply to celebrate an especially successful hunt. If a brave killed more game than his family could eat, he held a feast for all his friends and neighbors. Nobody was allowed to leave the feast until the last bit of food was gone. To make sure of this, the wigwam door was kept shut until there was nothing left to eat.

Many North American Indian tribes had groups, called societies, that played important roles at religious celebrations and festivals. The Iroquois had a False Face Society. The braves in this group wore weirdly carved masks during their ceremony. The ceremony of the False Face Society was done in hopes of protecting people from evil and curing diseases.

16

Among the tribes of the Southeast, the Muskhogeans were divided into a red clan and a white clan. The Muskhogeans wore body paints at religious festivals and at the *busk*. The busk was the mid-summer Green Corn Feast of the Southeast's farming tribes.

At every busk the clans played each other in a huge game of lacrosse. The team that first scored twenty points was the winner. After the game, the winning team marched around its goal in triumph, then held a spirited dance called the Stomp Dance.

Among the Plains Indians, who lived on the prairie lands between the Mississippi River and the Rocky Mountains, the main festival was the Sun Dance. Some of the Plains tribes held their Sun Dance as the winter was ending. Others celebrated the festival in mid-summer, before the great fall buffalo hunt. But the ceremony was just about the same for all the Plains tribes.

Priest using eagle-wing whistle during Shoshoni Sun Dance.

Long before the festival took place, one of
the tribal chiefs was chosen as religious
leader for that particular Sun Dance. That
chief picked the place where the dance
would be held. The location had to have a
good supply of wood for cooking fires,
water for people and animals, and grass for
the horses.

Once the Sun Dance leader chose a location, he revealed it to a number of young braves. Their job was to ride out and tell all the families of the tribe when and where the festival would be held. This was done far in advance, because the braves had to ride very slowly. The Plains Indians believed that sacred things must never be done hurriedly.

The actual Sun Dance festival lasted about twelve days. The first four days were devoted to traveling and setting up teepees at the festival place. For the Sun Dance, the teepees were arranged in a large circle, with the openings facing the center. At all other times, the Plains Indians arranged their teepees in lines, with the openings facing east.

The next four days were called the Getting Ready Time. During this period the ceremonial lodge was built. A tall, broad tree trunk was erected in the center. The lodge walls were made of smaller logs, set in a circle about forty feet across and covered with green willow branches. The Getting Ready Time was also an occasion for feasts, games, and sports competitions. Everyone took part in these ceremonies.

The final four days were devoted to the Sun Dance itself. In the Sun Dance, the braves danced around the center pole of the lodge for many hours. As they danced, they stuck sharp sticks into their skin. At no time did the dancers show their pain or weariness, even though they bled and suffered greatly. The dance symbolized the struggle of the human soul to free itself from the bonds of the body. The scars that resulted from the Sun Dance were worn proudly by the Indians. They were like badges of honor.

Green Corn Dance

The Pueblo Indians of the Southwest were primarily farmers, so their many rituals and festivals were connected with the seasons, the rains, and the harvests.

One of the most important Pueblo festivals was the Green Corn Dance. It was held in August, when the corn was ripening on the stalks. The festival was a way of thanking the spirits for the corn. It was also a time to ask the rain gods, called Kachinas, for rain to assure a good harvest.

24

The festival opened with prayers and dances in the kiva. A kiva was a kind of temple. It was a large, circular room, built partly or completely underground. The door to the kiva was a square opening in the roof. It symbolized the hole through which the first people were said to have emerged from the earth. Little is known about these indoor ceremonies, because generations of Pueblo Indians have kept them secret.

After the ceremonies in the kiva were ended, outdoor dances began in the village. The music for the dances was made by drums, rattles, sticks that were rubbed together, and singers. Dancing continued all day and did not stop until feasting began at night.

The Indians who lived in California did not farm or hunt. They lived almost entirely on acorns that were gathered from trees. But while their lives were easy and peaceful, their festivals were almost totally concerned with death.

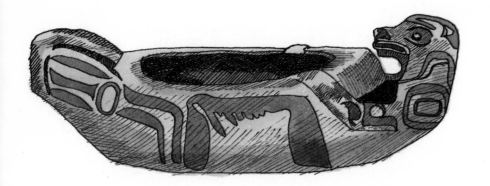

Every year, on the anniversary of a death, relatives of the dead person gave gifts to other members of the tribe and held feasts with dancing. The dead person's name was never spoken, since that would bring bad luck.

The Indians of the Northwest Coast of North America held great festivals, called potlatches. Potlatches celebrated marriages, births, and deaths, and they were held to show off wealth and to repay debts.

A potlatch began with several days of feasting. Then the host would praise himself and brag about his possessions. After that, he would begin giving away his possessions. Guests who took home gifts from a potlatch repaid the host at a potlatch of their own.

29

Kwakiutl potlatch

In time, the tribes of the Northwest—like those in the rest of North America—lost their lands to the settlers. And with the land went the way of life the Indians had followed for many centuries. The great festivals were no longer held.

Today, however, Indians of many different tribes are seeking to revive the memorable festivals of their ancestors—the proud traditions of the past.